AMAZING ORiGAMi

Floating Origami

Joe Fullman

Gareth Stevens
PUBLISHING

Please visit our website, www.garethstevens.com. For a free color catalog of all our high-quality books, call toll free 1-800-542-2595 or fax 1-877-542-2596.

Cataloging-in-Publication Data
Fullman, Joe.
Floating origami / by Joe Fullman.
p. cm. — (Amazing origami)
Includes index.
ISBN 978-1-4824-4171-0 (pbk.)
ISBN 978-1-4824-4172-7 (6-pack)
ISBN 978-1-4824-4167-3 (library binding)
1. Origami — Juvenile literature. 2. Sea in art — Juvenile literature.
I. Fullman, Joe. II. Title.
TT870.F85 2016
736'.982—d23

First Edition

Published in 2016 by
Gareth Stevens Publishing
111 East 14th Street, Suite 349
New York, NY 10003

Models and photography: Belinda Webster and Michael Wiles
Text: Joe Fullman
Design: Emma Randall
Editor: Frances Evans

Printed in the United States of America
CPSIA compliance information: Batch CW16GS: For further information contact Gareth Stevens, New York, New York at 1-800-542-2595.

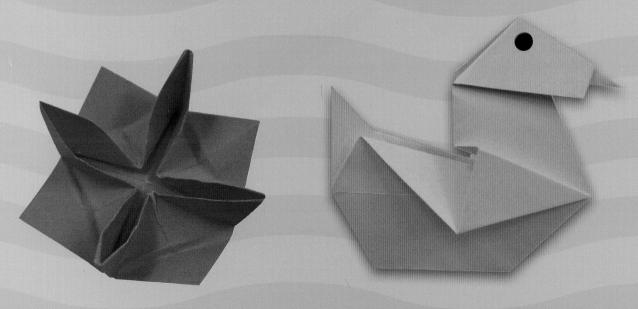

Contents

Basic Folds 4

Catamaran 6

Lotus Flower 10

Canoe 14

Steamboat 18

Duckling 22

Motorboat 28

Glossary, Further Reading, and Index 32

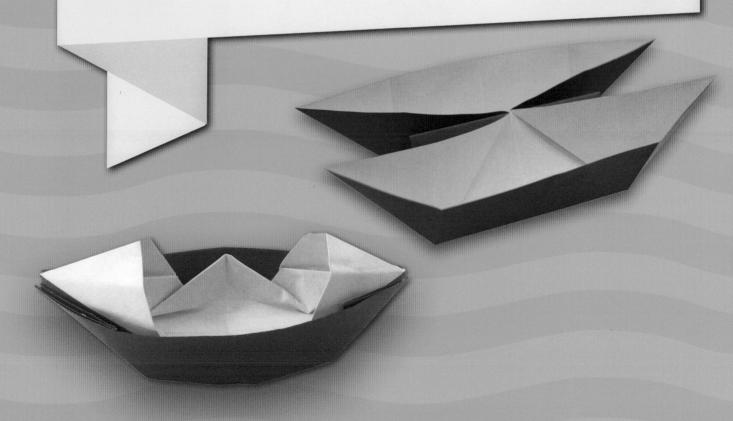

Basic Folds

Origami has been popular in Japan for hundreds of years and is now loved all around the world. You can make great models with just one sheet of paper... and this book shows you how!

The paper used in origami is thin but strong, so that it can be folded many times. It is usually colored on one side. Alternatively you can use ordinary scrap paper, but make sure it's not too thick.

Origami models often share the same folds and basic designs. This introduction explains some of the folds that you will need for the projects in this book, and they will also come in useful if you make other origami models. When making the models in this book, follow the key below to find out what the lines and arrows mean. And always crease well!

KEY

valley fold - - - - - - - - - -

mountain fold ....

step fold (mountain and valley fold next to each other)

direction to move paper

push ◀

MOUNTAIN FOLD

To make a mountain fold, fold the paper so that the crease is pointing up towards you, like a mountain.

VALLEY FOLD

To make a valley fold, fold the paper the other way, so that the crease is pointing away from you, like a valley.

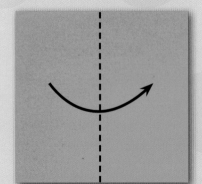

A NOTE ABOUT MEASUREMENTS

Measurements are given in U.S. form with the metric in parentheses. The metric conversion is rounded to make it easier to measure.

INSIDE REVERSE FOLD

An inside reverse fold is useful if you want to make a nose or a tail, or if you want to flatten off the shape of another part of an origami model.

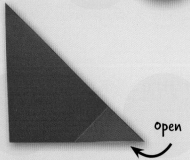

Open

1 Practice by first folding a piece of paper diagonally in half. Make a valley fold on one point and crease.

2 It's important to make sure that the paper is creased well. Run your finger over the crease two or three times.

3 Unfold and open up the corner slightly. Refold the crease nearest to you into a mountain fold.

4 Open up the paper a little more and then tuck the tip of the point inside. Close the paper. This is the view from the underside of the paper.

5 Flatten the paper. You now have an inside reverse fold.

OUTSIDE REVERSE FOLD

An outside reverse fold is useful if you want to make a head, beak or foot, or another part of your model that sticks out.

1 Practice by first folding a piece of paper diagonally in half. Make a valley fold on one point and crease.

2 It's important to make sure that the paper is creased well. Run your finger over the crease two or three times.

3 Unfold and open up the corner slightly. Refold the crease furthest away from you into a valley fold.

Open

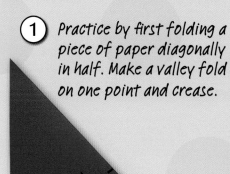

4 Open up the paper a little more and start to turn the corner inside out. Then close the paper when the fold begins to turn.

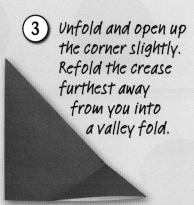

5 You now have an outside reverse fold. You can either flatten the paper or leave it rounded out.

Catamaran

A catamaran is a special type of boat with two long, equal-sized hulls. That means this origami catamaran has twice the floating power of a normal boat!

1. Place your paper white side up, like this. Valley fold it in half from left to right.

2. Fold the paper in half again from left to right.

3. Your paper should look like this. Unfold and rotate the paper 90° couterclockwise so the fold lines are horizontal.

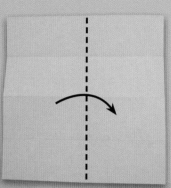

4. Valley fold the paper in half from left to right.

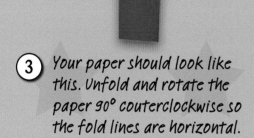

5. Again, valley fold the paper in half from left to right.

6. Your paper should look like this. Unfold it.

⑦ Diagonally fold the top left corner to the bottom right, and unfold. Then diagonally fold the top right corner to the bottom left, and unfold.

⑧ Valley fold the right edge to the center.

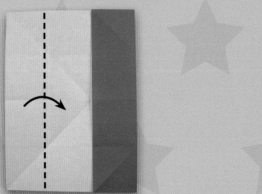

⑨ Valley fold the left edge to the center.

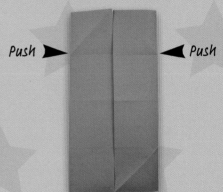

Push ▶   ◀ Push

⑩ Push out the folds at the top of the paper.

Did You Know?

The first catamarans were made of tree trunks over 2,000 years ago in Polynesia. The people used them to travel thousands of miles between islands.

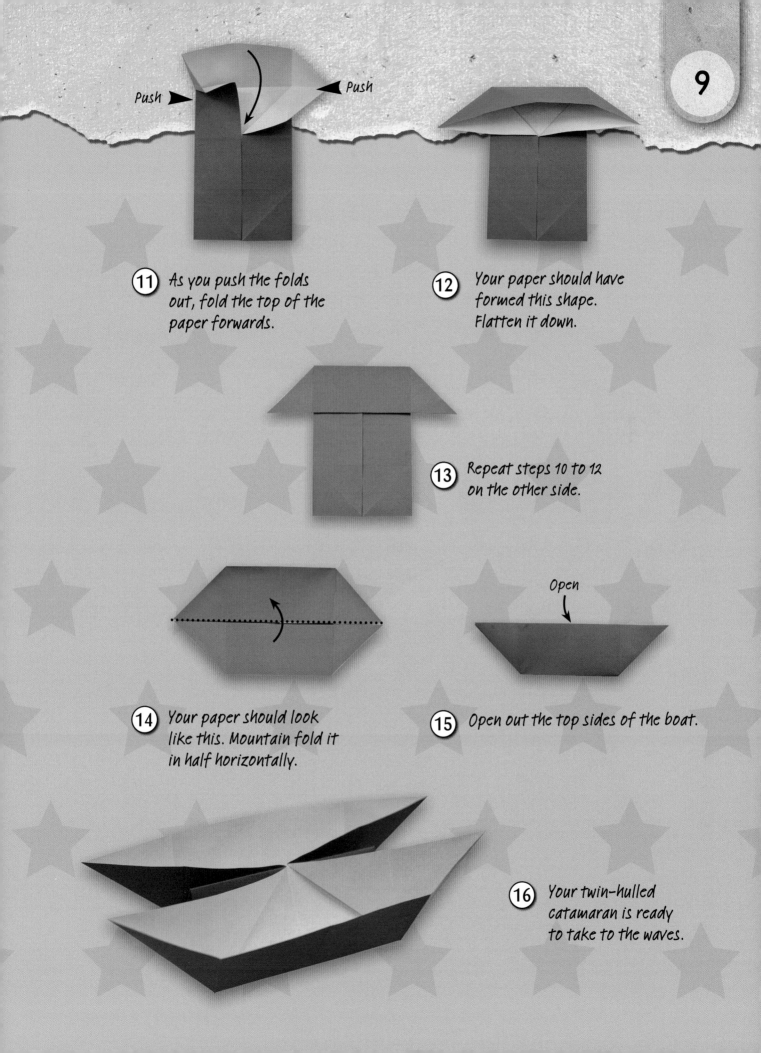

Push ◄   ► Push

11 As you push the folds out, fold the top of the paper forwards.

12 Your paper should have formed this shape. Flatten it down.

13 Repeat steps 10 to 12 on the other side.

14 Your paper should look like this. Mountain fold it in half horizontally.

Open

15 Open out the top sides of the boat.

16 Your twin-hulled catamaran is ready to take to the waves.

Lotus Flower

Medium

The lotus is a beautiful flower from Asia. It grows in water, floating on the surface. This project will require some strong finger power, as you'll need to fold the paper over several times.

1. Place the paper white side up, with one corner facing you. Make two valley folds as shown, then unfold.

2. Valley fold the left corner to the center line.

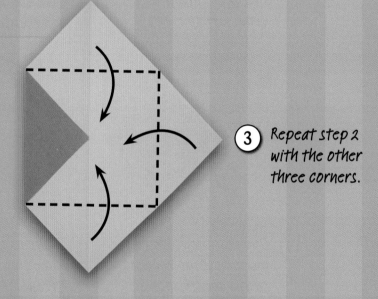

3. Repeat step 2 with the other three corners.

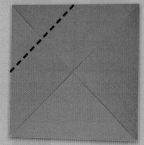

4. Fold the top left corner to the center line.

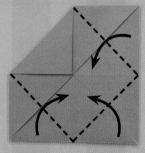

5. Repeat step 4 with the other 3 corners.

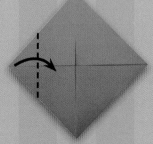

6. Again, fold the left corner to the center line.

Did You Know?

The lotus is an important flower in the Hindu religion, and is associated with many gods. The lotus is also the national flower of India.

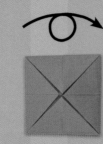

7 Repeat step 6 with the other 3 corners.

8 Your paper should look like this. Turn it over from left to right.

9 For the final time, fold the top left corner to the center point.

10 Repeat step 9 with the other 3 sides.

11 Open up the folds you made in steps 9 and 10, so the corners point outwards.

12 Your paper should look like this. Turn it over from left to right.

13 Unfold the top center point up to the top.

14 Repeat step 13 with the other three center points.

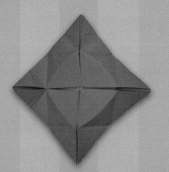

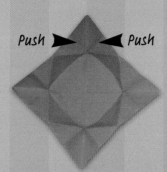

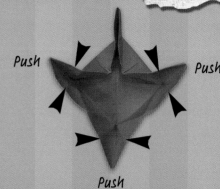

(15) Your paper should look like this. Turn it over from right to left.

(16) Push the top points together. The other points will begin to come together too.

(17) Push the other three points together.

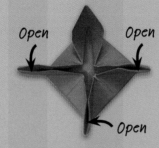

(18) Push open the top point of the model to form a rounded, petal-like shape.

(19) Push open the other three points to form petal shapes.

(20) Your paper should look like this. Gently reach under the paper and unfold the point beneath the top left edge.

(21) Repeat step 20 with the other 3 edges.

(22) Plump out your petals and your lotus is ready to float.

Canoe

A canoe is a lightweight, open-top boat. People use canoes for fishing and for racing down fast white-water courses. How will you use yours?

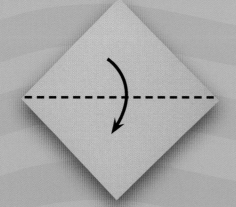

① Place your paper white side up with a corner facing you. Valley fold it in half from top to bottom.

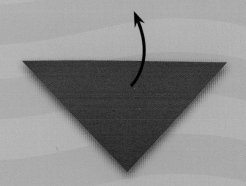

② Unfold the paper.

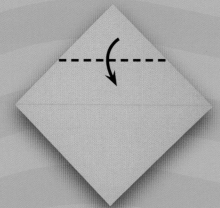

③ Fold the top corner to the center.

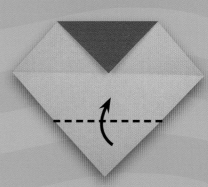

④ Fold the bottom corner to the center.

⑤ Valley fold the top edge to the central fold line.

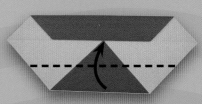

⑥ Valley fold the bottom edge to the central fold line.

7 Fold the left point to the right, as shown.

8 Fold the right point to the left, as shown.

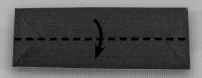

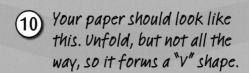

9 Valley fold the paper in half from top to bottom.

10 Your paper should look like this. Unfold, but not all the way, so it forms a "V" shape.

Did You Know?

In 1986, Don Starkell and his son Dana paddled 12,000 miles from their home in the United States to the Amazon River in South America – the longest canoe journey ever!

Push ► ◄ Push

Tuck

⑪ Push the folds on the right-
and left-hand sides inwards
so they go in towards the
center of the boat.

⑫ Tuck the raised right-hand
point inside the long flap
above it.

► Push

Tuck

⑬ As you tuck, the bottom side will
form a curved pointed shape.
Keep pushing until the point is
all the way inside the flap.

⑭ Your paper should look like
this. Now repeat steps 12 and
13 on the other side.

⑮ It's time to paddle your canoe!

Steamboat

Medium

More than one hundred years ago, the world's biggest boats were powered by giant steam engines and had huge chimneys that released great clouds of smoke. Have a go at making one of your own.

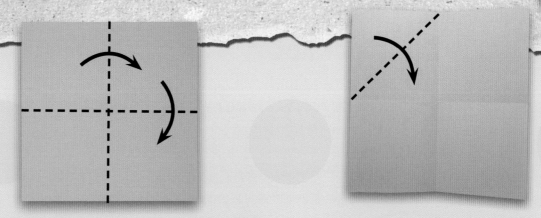

1. Place the paper as shown. Valley fold it in half from top to bottom, and unfold. Then valley fold it in half from left to right, and unfold.

2. Fold the top left corner to the center.

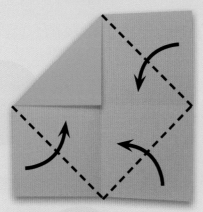

3. Repeat step 2 with the other three corners.

4. Your paper should look like this. Turn it over from left to right.

5. Fold the left corner to the center.

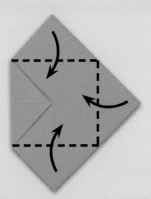

6. Repeat step 5 with the other three corners.

(7) Your paper should look like this. Turn it over from left to right.

(8) Again, fold the top left corner to the center.

(9) Repeat step 8 with the other three corners.

(10) Your paper should look like this. Turn it over from left to right.

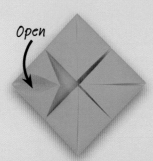

Open

(11) Open out the left-hand side until it starts to form a mouth shape, like this.

Push

(12) Push to the left to form a rectangle, but keep the pocket open. This is your first chimney.

Open

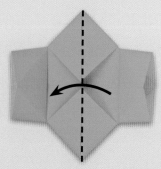

(13) Repeat steps 11 and 12 on the right-hand side to form your other chimney.

(14) Your paper should look like this. Make a horizontal valley fold from right to left, then unfold.

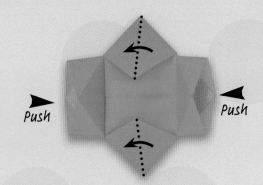

Push

Push

(15) Make mountain folds at the top and bottom, like this, and start pushing the two sides of the paper together.

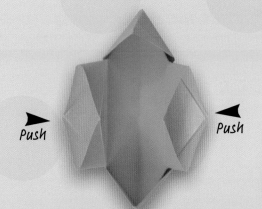

Push

Push

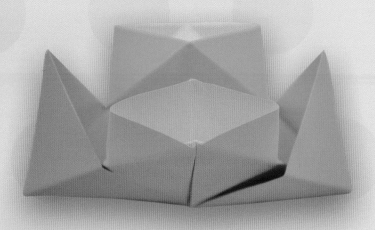

(16) The paper should start to rise up, bringing the chimneys together and forming the shape of your boat.

(17) Your steamboat is ready. Fire up the engines and it's anchors aweigh!

Duckling

Quack quack! Here comes an origami duckling paddling along the water. Why not make a whole family of ducks and take them all for a swim together?

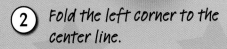

1 With your paper white side up and a corner facing you, make a valley fold from left to right, then unfold.

2 Fold the left corner to the center line.

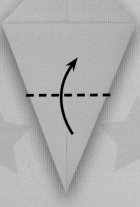

3 Fold the right corner to the center line.

4 Fold the bottom point up to the top.

5 Fold the bottom left corner over to the center line.

6 Fold the bottom right corner over to the center line.

⑦ Open out the folds you made in steps 5 and 6.

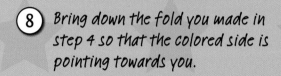

⑧ Bring down the fold you made in step 4 so that the colored side is pointing towards you.

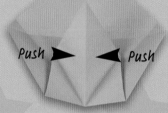

Push ▶ ◀ Push

⑨ Your paper should look like this. As you bring the point forward, press its sides together.

⑩ When the point is sticking straight at you, valley fold the whole paper in half from right to left.

⑪ Then make a diagonal valley fold as shown.

⑫ Now turn the fold you made in step 11 into a mountain fold as well.

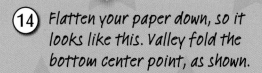

Push

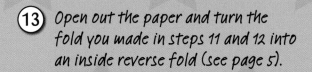

13 Open out the paper and turn the fold you made in steps 11 and 12 into an inside reverse fold (see page 5).

14 Flatten your paper down, so it looks like this. Valley fold the bottom center point, as shown.

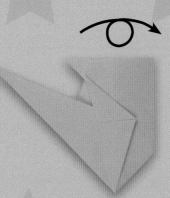

15 Your paper should look like this. Turn it over from left to right, and repeat step 14 on the other side.

16 Your paper should look like this. Make a small valley fold on the top layer of paper.

17 Now fold the corner you just made the other way, as a mountain fold, and tuck it behind so it's out of sight. Then turn the paper over from left to right, and repeat steps 16 and 17 on the other side.

18 Your paper should look like this. Make another small valley fold, as shown.

19 Fold the corner you just made the other way, as a mountain fold, and tuck it behind so it's out of sight. Turn the paper over and repeat steps 18 and 19 on the other side.

20 Your paper should look like this. Fold down the right point, as shown.

21 Fold the point the other way to make a mountain fold. Then flip it over to make an outside reverse fold (see page 5).

22 Your paper should look like this. Flatten it down.

Did You Know?

Duck feathers have a waxy coating that makes them waterproof. So no matter how long they spend in the water, ducks never really get wet.

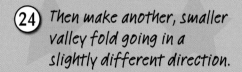

23 Make a valley fold along the top section, as shown.

24 Then make another, smaller valley fold going in a slightly different direction.

Open

25 Now turn the folds from steps 23 and 24 into two inside reverse folds, one inside the other (see page 5).

26 Your duckling is almost done. Open up its wings.

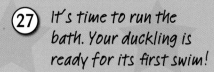

27 It's time to run the bath. Your duckling is ready for its first swim!

Motorboat

The motorboat is the fastest of all boats, zipping across the water at great speeds. Here's how to make a sleek and streamlined origami version.

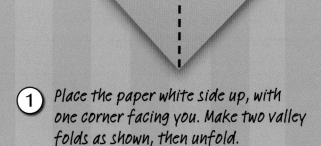

1 Place the paper white side up, with one corner facing you. Make two valley folds as shown, then unfold.

2 Valley fold the left corner to the center line.

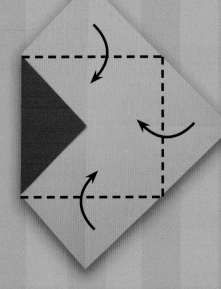

3 Repeat step 2 with the other three corners.

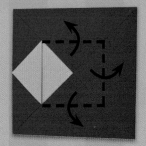

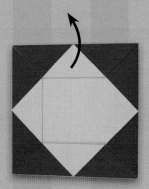

4 Take the central left-hand point and valley fold it back to the left.

5 Repeat step 4 with the other three central points, as shown.

6 Your paper should now look like this. Unfold the top side.

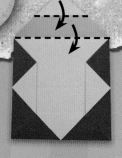

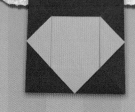

7 Fold forward the top point, then fold it over again so the point is hidden.

8 Repeat steps 6 and 7 with the bottom side.

9 Mountain fold the top section back, as shown.

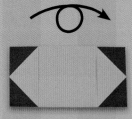

10 Mountain fold the bottom section back.

11 Your paper should look like this. Turn it over from left to right.

12 Fold the top right corner down to the central line.

13 Repeat step 12 with the other 3 corners.

14 Fold the top right corner down, as shown.

15 Repeat step 14 with the other three corners.

Did You Know?

In 1978, the Australian Ken Warby set the water speed record, racing at over 317 mph (511 kph) in a boat, the *Spirit of Australia*, that he'd built in his backyard.

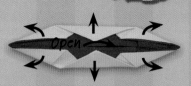

(16) Fold the top point down to the center.

(17) Fold the bottom point up to the center.

(18) Unfold the folds made in steps 14 to 17 and start to open up the central horizontal folds.

(19) Your paper should look like this. Keep opening up the central folds.

(20) When the folds are wide apart, like this, push the model up from below to turn the boat inside out, so that the colored side bulges outwards.

(21) Your paper should look like this. Turn it over from left to right.

(22) Lift up the white fold of paper on the left side.

(23) Now open up the white fold of paper on the right side.

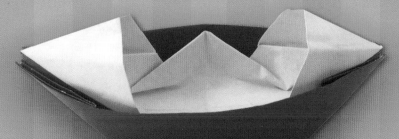

(24) Your motorboat is ready to race.

Glossary

catamaran A boat with two hulls that are the same size.

crease A line in a piece of paper made by folding.

Hinduism The main religion of India. Among other things, followers of Hinduism believe in many gods and that after you die you return to life in a different form.

hull The main body of a boat.

iceberg A large piece of ice that has broken away from a glacier and is floating at sea.

lotus A type of water lily.

mountain fold An origami step where a piece of paper is folded so that the crease is pointing upwards, like a mountain.

Polynesia A group of islands in the central and southern Pacific Ocean.

step fold A mountain fold and valley fold next to each other.

streamlined Designed to move as quickly as possible through air or water.

valley fold An origami step where a piece of paper is folded so that the crease is pointing downwards, like a valley.

Further Reading

Akass, Susan. *My First Origami Book*. Cico Kidz, 2011.

Ono, Mari. *Origami: Cars, Boats, Trains, and More*. Cico Books, 2014.

Robinson, Nick. *The Awesome Origami Pack*. Barron's Educational Series, Inc., 2014.

Index

B
boats 6, 9, 14, 17, 21, 28, 30

C
canoes 14-17
catamarans 6-9
chimneys 18, 20, 21

D
ducklings 22-27
ducks 22, 26

H
hulls 6, 9

I
inside reverse folds 5, 25, 27

L
lotus flowers 10-13

M
motorboats 28-31

O
outside reverse folds 5, 21

P
petals 13

S
Spirit of Australia 30
steamboats 18-21

T
Titanic 20